PRINCESS MARJABELLE
VISITS
LOLLYGAG LAKE

PRINCESS MARJABELLE
VISITS
LOLLYGAG LAKE

*Marjabelle Young Stewart's Introduction
to Manners for the Pre-Schooler*

Written by Nancy Nehlsen
With Marjabelle Young Stewart

Pictures by Sandra Carlson

Robert B. Luce, Inc.
PUBLISHERS

A dapper alligator helps two lazy Lollygaggers,
Hop T. Hop, the frog, and Water Pop, the turtle,
learn their manners in time to meet a very
proper Princess.

PRINCESS MARJABELLE VISITS LOLLYGAG LAKE

COPYRIGHT © 1994 BY MARJABELLE YOUNG STEWART
AND NANCY NEHLSEN

LIBRARY OF CONGRESS CATALOGUE NUMBER: 93-85903

ISBN: 0–88331–214–X

MANUFACTURED IN SINGAPORE

1 2 3 4 5

Special thanks
to Alex McWhorter
for his characters
Hop T. Hop,
Water Pop
and
Hank U. Alligator.

PRINCESS MARJABELLE
VISITS
LOLLYGAG LAKE

Hop T. Hop and Water Pop spent lazy days lying on lily pads in Lollygag Lake, spitting long streams of water at each other and burping bubbles in the water.

Life had always been lazy at Lollygag Lake. Everyone who was born there spent their lives lying around on lily pads watching the time go by.

Everyone, that is, except Hank U. Alligator! Hank U. was different. He never burped. He never spit. He was always polite. Hank U. was very different from the other residents of Lollygag Lake, but no one really knew how he got that way. When Hank U. walked by, Hop T. Hop and Water Pop would just roll their eyes and say, "Well, there goes Mr. Manners. Who would want to be like him?"

And then Hop T. Hop and Water Pop would go right back to lazing away the day on their lily pads and waiting for a tasty fly to buzz by.

It wasn't until something really fantastic happened that life began to change for the two lazy friends. It started out like any other day, until, suddenly, Hop T. Hop and Water Pop heard the excited fluttering of wings nearby. It was Florene Butterfly and she was very excited.

"Don't just flutter by, Miss Butterfly," said Hop T. Hop. "Tell us what all the excitement is about."

"Princess Marjabelle, ruler of all the nearby lakes and rivers, ponds and swamps, is coming HERE, to Lollygag Lake," she answered in her shrill, high voice. "And everyone—I mean, EVERYONE—even the lazy likes of you, must be ready to greet her."

Water Pop's mouth dropped open and Hop T. Hop's tongue tumbled right out of his mouth and onto his lily pad.

"Why, we've never met a Princess before. How will we act? What will we say?" they both asked, speaking at the same time.

"Well, I don't know, but I do know you'd better find out or you'll look pretty silly to the Princess." And off fluttered Florene Butterfly, muttering to herself.

The two friends stared at each other. "What will we do?" Suddenly they croaked together, "Hank U. Alligator! Yes, we'll get Hank U. to teach us how to act for a Princess." And off they hopped to the home of Hank U. Alligator.

Sheepishly they knocked on his door. Hank U. opened the door wide, smiled warmly at the two and said, "Why Hop T. Hop and Water Pop, how do you do? It's so nice to see you. Won't you come in?"

The two pushed shyly through Hank U.'s door. "How may I help you?" Hank U. offered brightly.

Staring at the floor, the two began to mumble, "Uh, well, we . . . Princess Marjabelle is . . . you see . . . we don't know much about . . . I mean, we've never been out of . . . it's just that . . ."

"We don't know how to act," Hop T. finally said.

Hank U. smiled. "I understand perfectly. You want to make a good impression on the Princess. I'd be delighted to help. Now let's get started, shall we? There's not much time before the Princess arrives."

Hop T. Hop and Water Pop sat very still and listened.

"Now, when you're introduced, what do you do?"

The two looked at each other, dropped their heads and stared at the floor. "No, no, that won't do," Hank U. said, shaking his head.

"You must pull yourself straight up, look her right in the eye and say with a smile, 'How do you do, Your Majesty. I'm delighted to meet you.' When she extends her hand, take hold with your right hand and give her a good strong handshake. Here, hold your hand out straight like a gun, put your web in my paw and give it a try."

At first the two felt silly, shaking hands and saying, "How do you do? So nice to meet you."

But soon they were smiling broadly as they practiced grasping Hank U.'s paw firmly and giving it a shake.

"Next," Hank U said, "you must remember to say 'please' when you ask for something and 'thank you' when someone gives you something, even if it's a compliment." Hop T. Hop and Water Pop practiced saying "please" and "thank you". "Cover your mouth if you yawn, cough or sneeze. Say 'pardon me' when you walk in front of someone. Call the Princess, 'Your Majesty', but all other adults, 'Ma'am' or 'Sir'. Say, 'Excuse me, please' when you're leaving the room."

Water Pop's head began to swim. And Hop T. Hop had to sit down for a moment to take it all in.

"I'm afraid we'll never be ready to meet the Princess," he sighed. "You see, Hank U., we're just not like you." The two friends shook their heads sadly. "We are plain and simple, lazy old Lollygaggers," said Hop T. Hop, "who don't fit in with fancy alligators or Princesses. I believe the best place for us to be when the Princess comes is under our lily pads where she won't see us."

"Nonsense!" bellowed Hank U. Alligator, in a most alligatorish voice. "Anyone can have manners and everyone SHOULD. Why, all you have to do is follow a few simple rules. 'Please' when you want something. 'Thank you' when you get it. 'How do you do?' when you meet someone. 'Excuse me' when you're leaving."

Hop T. Hop and Water Pop jumped to their feet. "We always cover our mouths if we yawn, cough or sneeze. We shake hands firmly and say 'pardon me' if we walk in front of someone."

"Good," bellowed Hank U. "Now let's go on. When you're invited to dine with the Princess and you don't like what she serves, you may never say 'yuck' or 'ick' or 'don't you have a fresh fly?' You must smile, take a small bite and push your food around on your plate so no one sees that you are displeased.

Always treat everyone in the way you want to be treated. And,
the most important rule of all—see the good in yourself and
show it to everyone. That way, everyone will feel comfortable and
you will always fit in."

Hop T. Hop and Water Pop shook their heads happily. "I think
we can do it! I KNOW we can do it!"

The next afternoon Princess Marjabelle arrived at Lollygag Lake. Hop T. Hop and Water Pop waited nervously for their turn to meet the lovely Princess. "Thank you, please, pardon me, excuse me, how do you do, so nice to meet you," Water Pop muttered under his breath.

"Sshh," whispered Hop T. Hop, "she's almost here. Stop practicing and start smiling."

At that moment the Princess held out a tiny gloved hand to Water Pop. He pulled himself up, looked her straight in the eye, shook her hand firmly, smiled a big smile and said politely, "How do you do, Your Majesty. I'm delighted to meet you."

Hop T. Hop followed. "How do you do, Your Majesty. I'm delighted to meet you."

The Princess smiled and touched their heads. "You are fine fellows," she said. "I did not realize what wonderful manners you Lollygaggers have. We must invite you to dine at Polliwog Palace."

Hop T. Hop and Water Pop swelled with pride. "We fit in anywhere now," they told each other. "We must find Hank U. and tell him."

Hank U. Alligator greeted them at his door.

"Hank U.!" they bubbled. "You made us into fine fellows. That's exactly what the Princess said. She said we're FINE FELLOWS!"

Hank U. smiled broadly. "Of course she did. But you did it yourselves. I just gave you the rules. You learned them well, you used them, and now everyone can see what fine fellows you are. You acted as if you fit in with the best—and now you do."

"We did do it, didn't we?" giggled Hop T. Hop. He held out his arm to Water Pop.

"Please," he said.

Water Pop took his arm. "Thank you," he said.

Then they both turned to Hank U. Alligator and said politely,
"Excuse us, please." Then the two fine friends from Lollygag
Lake hopped off into the world to do what all fine fellows do.